HOW TO BECOME WEALTHY FROM NOTHING

An Essential Guide To Financial Success, Personal Fulfillment And Beyond

Spencer Ryan Maxwell

Table of Contents

INTRODUCTION 4
CHAPTER ONE 14
   MINDSET AND ATTITUDE 14
CHAPTER TWO 22
   FINANCIAL EDUCATION 22
CHAPTER THREE 31
   CREATING A BUDGET 31
CHAPTER FOUR 40
   SAVING MONEY 40
CHAPTER FIVE 50
   DEBT MANAGEMENT 50
CHAPTER SIX 60
   INCREASING YOUR INCOME 60
CHAPTER SEVEN 69
   INVESTING 69
CHAPTER EIGHT 80
   BUILDING PASSIVE INCOME 80
CHAPTER NINE 90
   ENTREPRENEURSHIP 90
CHAPTER TEN 102
   NETWORKING AND MENTORSHIP 102
CHAPTER ELEVEN 112
   FRUGALITY AND SMART SPENDING 112
CHAPTER TWELVE 122

CONTINUOUS LEARNING AND ADAPTATION 122
CHAPTER THIRTEEN 132
    PHILANTHROPY AND GIVING BACK 132
THE END 140

INTRODUCTION
The Journey to Wealth

Embarking on the journey to wealth can seem daunting, especially if you are starting from scratch. However, becoming wealthy is not just about having a lot of money; it's about understanding and implementing certain principles and strategies that can help you build and sustain wealth over time. The journey to wealth involves a combination of smart financial management, disciplined habits, continuous learning, and a proactive approach to opportunities.

When we talk about wealth, it's important to realize that it's a marathon, not a sprint. Building wealth usually doesn't happen overnight. It requires patience, persistence, and a willingness to adapt and change your strategies as you learn and grow. The first step is to define what wealth means to you personally. For some, it might mean financial independence and freedom to make choices without worrying about money. For others, it might mean having enough resources to provide for their family and future generations.

Understanding that wealth goes beyond just money is crucial. It encompasses financial security, peace of mind, and the ability to live life on your terms. The journey to wealth also involves setting clear and realistic financial goals. These goals act as a roadmap, guiding your actions and decisions along the way. Whether it's saving for retirement, buying a home, or starting a business, having specific goals helps keep you focused and motivated.

An essential part of this journey is financial education. Understanding basic concepts like budgeting, saving, investing, and managing debt is fundamental. Equipping yourself with financial knowledge empowers you to make informed decisions and avoid common pitfalls. It's also beneficial to stay informed about economic trends and changes in the financial landscape. This awareness can help you make timely adjustments to your financial plan and capitalize on new opportunities.

One of the first practical steps on this journey is creating a budget. A budget helps you understand where your money is going and where you can cut back to save more. It's important to be honest with yourself about your spending habits and to prioritize your needs over your wants. Saving money is another cornerstone of wealth building. Establishing an emergency fund should be one of your initial financial goals. This fund acts as a safety net, providing financial security and peace of mind in case of unexpected expenses.

Managing debt effectively is another critical aspect. Debt can be a major obstacle to building wealth, but with careful planning and discipline, it can be managed and eventually eliminated. It's important to understand the different types of debt, such as good debt (like a mortgage or student loan) and bad debt (like credit card debt). Developing a strategy to pay off high-interest debt first can save you money in the long run and help you become debt-free faster.

Increasing your income is another important step. This can be achieved through various means such as finding a side hustle, negotiating a raise at your current job, or exploring new career opportunities that offer higher pay. Building multiple streams of income not only increases your financial stability but also accelerates your wealth-building process.

Investing is a powerful tool for growing your wealth. Understanding the basics of investing and building a diversified portfolio can help you achieve higher returns on your money over time. It's important to start early and invest consistently, even if you can only afford to invest a small amount initially. The power of compound interest can significantly boost your wealth over the long term.

Building passive income streams is another effective way to achieve financial independence. Passive income is money earned with little to no effort on your part. Examples include rental income, dividends from investments, or royalties from creative work. These income streams can provide financial stability and freedom, allowing you to focus on other pursuits.

Understanding Wealth: Beyond Money

Wealth is often perceived solely in terms of monetary assets, but true wealth extends far beyond financial riches. It encompasses various aspects of life that contribute to overall well-being and fulfillment. Understanding wealth in a broader sense involves recognizing the importance of health, relationships, personal growth, and time freedom.

Health is a fundamental component of wealth. Without good health, it becomes challenging to enjoy any financial success. Investing in your physical and mental well-being through regular exercise, a balanced diet, and stress management is crucial. Healthy individuals are more productive, have more energy, and can make better decisions, which positively impacts their financial journey.

Relationships and social connections also play a significant role in overall wealth. Building and maintaining strong, supportive relationships with family, friends, and colleagues can provide emotional support, guidance, and opportunities for collaboration. A robust social network can open doors to new opportunities, both personally and professionally.

Personal growth and continuous learning are vital for a fulfilling life. Investing in your education and skills can lead to better job prospects, higher earning potential, and greater career satisfaction. It also keeps you adaptable in a constantly changing world, allowing you to seize new opportunities as they arise.

Time freedom is another critical aspect of wealth. Having the flexibility to spend your time as you wish, whether it's pursuing hobbies, traveling, or spending quality time with loved ones, is invaluable. Achieving financial independence can grant you the freedom to prioritize what truly matters to you, rather than being tied to a demanding job or financial worries.

CHAPTER ONE

MINDSET AND ATTITUDE
Developing a Wealth Mindset

A wealth mindset is the foundation for building and maintaining financial success. It involves a set of attitudes, beliefs, and behaviors that help you think and act in ways that promote financial growth and stability. Developing a wealth mindset starts with the recognition that wealth is not just about having money, but also about creating value, making wise choices, and continuously improving your financial knowledge and skills.

One of the key aspects of a wealth mindset is thinking long-term. Instead of focusing on immediate gratification, people with a wealth mindset plan for the future and make decisions that will benefit them in the long run. This might involve saving money, investing in education or training, and setting aside funds for retirement.

Another important element is being proactive. Those with a wealth mindset take control of their financial situation rather than letting circumstances dictate their financial health. This means actively seeking opportunities to increase income, reduce expenses, and invest wisely. They also regularly review and adjust their financial plans to stay on track toward their goals.

Positivity and optimism are also crucial. A positive outlook helps you stay motivated and resilient in the face of challenges. Believing in your ability to achieve financial success can drive you to take the necessary steps to improve your financial situation. It's important to celebrate small victories along the way and to view setbacks as learning opportunities rather than failures.

Overcoming Limiting Beliefs

Limiting beliefs are negative thoughts and attitudes that hold you back from achieving your full potential. When it comes to building wealth, common limiting beliefs include thoughts like "I'll never be able to save enough money," "Investing is too risky," or "I'm just not good with money." These beliefs can create mental barriers that prevent you from taking action to improve your financial situation.

To overcome limiting beliefs, the first step is to identify them. Pay attention to the negative thoughts that arise when you think about money and financial goals. Once you are aware of these beliefs, challenge them by asking yourself if they are really true. Often, these beliefs are based on past experiences or misconceptions rather than facts.

Replace limiting beliefs with empowering ones. For example, instead of thinking "I'll never be able to save enough money," tell yourself "I can start saving small amounts regularly, and over time, it will add up." Instead of

"Investing is too risky," think "I can learn about different investment options and choose those that align with my risk tolerance."

Visualization and affirmations can also help. Imagine yourself achieving your financial goals and living a life of financial freedom. Use positive affirmations like "I am capable of managing my money wisely" or "I am on my way to financial independence." These techniques can reprogram your mind to focus on possibilities rather than limitations.

Setting and Achieving Financial Goals

Setting financial goals is a crucial step in building wealth. Goals give you direction and a clear path to follow, making it easier to make financial decisions and measure your progress. Effective financial goals are specific, measurable, achievable, relevant, and time-bound (SMART).

Start by identifying what you want to achieve financially. This could be paying off debt, saving for a down payment on a house, building an emergency fund, or investing for retirement. Be specific about what you want to accomplish. For example, instead of saying "I want to save money," set a goal like "I want to save $5,000 for an emergency fund within the next 12 months."

Next, break down your goals into smaller, manageable steps. If your goal is to save $5,000 in a year, figure out how much you need to save each month or each paycheck to reach that target. This makes the goal less overwhelming and more achievable.

Track your progress regularly. Keeping an eye on your progress helps you stay motivated and allows you to make adjustments if necessary. If you find that you are not on track to meet your goal, reassess your budget and spending habits to see where you can make changes.

It's also important to prioritize your goals. You may have multiple financial goals, but trying to achieve them all at once can be challenging. Decide which goals are most important and focus on those first. Once you achieve one goal, you can move on to the next.

Stay flexible and adaptable. Life is unpredictable, and your financial situation can change. Be prepared to adjust your goals and plans as needed. The key is to stay committed to your overall vision of financial success and to keep moving forward, even if the path changes along the way.

CHAPTER TWO

FINANCIAL EDUCATION
Basics of Personal Finance

Personal finance is the management of your money, including income, expenses, saving, investing, and planning for the future. Understanding the basics of personal finance is crucial for achieving financial stability and building wealth. Here are some key components:

1. Budgeting: Creating a budget helps you track your income and expenses. It allows you to see where your money is going and make adjustments to ensure you're living within your means. A budget typically includes categories for housing, utilities, groceries,

transportation, entertainment, and savings.

2. Saving: Saving money is essential for financial security. It provides a cushion for emergencies, helps you achieve financial goals, and prepares you for retirement. Aim to save a portion of your income regularly, even if it's a small amount.

3. Investing: Investing involves putting your money into assets like stocks, bonds, or real estate with the expectation of earning a return. It's a way to grow your wealth over time, but it also comes with risks. Understanding different types of investments and their risks is important.

4. Debt Management: Managing debt effectively means using credit responsibly and paying off debts promptly. Avoid high-interest debt, such as credit card debt, as it can quickly become unmanageable. Develop a plan to pay off any existing debt as soon as possible.

5. Financial Planning: Planning for the future involves setting financial goals and creating a strategy to achieve them. This might include saving for a house, paying for education, or planning for retirement. A financial plan helps you stay focused and make informed decisions.

Understanding Income and Expenses

Understanding your income and expenses is a fundamental part of managing your personal finances. Here's how to get a clear picture of your financial situation:

1. Income: Income is the money you receive, typically from your job, but it can also come from other sources like investments, side jobs, or government benefits. Make a list of all your income sources and the amount you receive from each.

2. Expenses: Expenses are the costs you incur for living. They can be categorized into fixed and variable expenses. Fixed expenses are consistent

and predictable, like rent or mortgage payments, utilities, and insurance premiums. Variable expenses fluctuate, such as groceries, entertainment, and dining out.

3. Tracking Expenses: Keep track of all your expenses to understand where your money is going. This can be done manually using a notebook, or digitally using budgeting apps or spreadsheets. Recording your expenses helps you identify spending patterns and areas where you can cut back.

4. Balancing Income and Expenses: Aim to spend less than you earn. If your expenses exceed your income, you need to either increase your income or reduce your expenses. Look for ways to cut

unnecessary spending, such as dining out less often, canceling unused subscriptions, or finding more affordable alternatives.

5. Creating a Surplus: A financial surplus means you have money left over after covering all your expenses. This surplus can be used for saving and investing, which are crucial for building wealth. Aim to increase your surplus by boosting your income and controlling your expenses.

The Power of Compound Interest

Compound interest is a powerful concept that can significantly boost your savings and investments over time. It's the interest earned on the initial principal, which also includes all the accumulated interest from previous periods. Here's how it works:

1. Simple Interest vs. Compound Interest: Simple interest is calculated only on the principal amount, whereas compound interest is calculated on the principal plus any previously earned interest. This means that with compound interest, you earn interest on your interest, which can lead to exponential growth.

2. How Compound Interest Works: Let's say you invest $1,000 at an annual interest rate of 5%. With simple interest, you'd earn $50 each year. However, with compound interest, you'd earn $50 the first year, and then in the second year, you'd earn interest on $1,050, resulting

in $52.50. Over time, this difference becomes substantial.

3.   The Rule of 72: The Rule of 72 is a simple way to estimate how long it will take for an investment to double with compound interest. Divide 72 by the annual interest rate. For example, if the interest rate is 6%, it will take approximately 12 years (72 ÷ 6) for your investment to double.

4.   Importance of Starting Early: The earlier you start investing, the more time your money has to grow through compound interest. Even small amounts can grow significantly over long periods. For example, if you invest $100 per month at an interest rate of 7%, you

could have around $120,000 after 30 years.

5. Consistent Investing: Regularly contributing to your savings and investments maximizes the benefits of compound interest. Consistent investing, even in small amounts, allows you to take full advantage of compounding.

CHAPTER THREE

CREATING A BUDGET

Importance of Budgeting

Budgeting is a crucial aspect of personal finance. It serves as a financial roadmap, helping you manage your money effectively, plan for future expenses, and achieve your financial goals. Here are some key reasons why budgeting is important:

1. Control Over Your Finances: Budgeting gives you a clear picture of your income and expenses, allowing you to make informed decisions about how to allocate your money. It helps prevent overspending and ensures that you live within your means.

2. Achieving Financial Goals: Whether you're saving for a big purchase, paying off debt, or planning for retirement, a budget helps you set and track financial goals. By knowing how much you can save each month, you can create a realistic plan to reach your objectives.

3. Emergency Preparedness: A budget helps you set aside money for emergencies. Having an emergency fund can provide financial security and peace of mind, enabling you to handle unexpected expenses without resorting to debt.

4. Reducing Financial Stress: Knowing exactly where your money is going can reduce financial stress and

anxiety. A budget helps you avoid surprises and ensures that you are prepared for both expected and unexpected expenses.

5. Building Better Habits: Budgeting encourages responsible spending and saving habits. It helps you prioritize your needs over your wants, making it easier to cut unnecessary expenses and focus on what truly matters.

How to Create a Personal Budget

Creating a personal budget involves several steps. Here's a simple guide to help you get started:

1. Determine Your Income: Calculate your total monthly income. This includes your salary, wages, bonuses, and any other sources of income like

freelance work or investments. Use your net income (after taxes) to get a more accurate picture of what you have available to spend.

2. List Your Expenses: Make a comprehensive list of all your monthly expenses. These can be categorized into fixed expenses (rent/mortgage, utilities, insurance, loan payments) and variable expenses (groceries, entertainment, dining out, transportation). Don't forget to include irregular expenses such as annual subscriptions or car maintenance.

3. Track Your Spending: For at least one month, track every dollar you spend. This helps you understand your spending habits and identify areas

where you might be overspending. You can do this manually with a notebook or use a budgeting app to simplify the process.

4. Set Financial Goals: Define your short-term and long-term financial goals. Short-term goals might include paying off a credit card or saving for a vacation, while long-term goals could be buying a house or building a retirement fund. Having clear goals will help you stay motivated and focused.

5. Create Your Budget: Based on your income and tracked expenses, allocate specific amounts for each expense category. Make sure your total expenses do not exceed your income. If they do,

you will need to adjust your spending to create a balanced budget.

6. Prioritize Savings: Make savings a priority by setting aside a portion of your income each month. Aim to save at least 20% of your income, but if that's not possible, start with a smaller percentage and gradually increase it.

7. Review and Adjust Regularly: Your budget is not set in stone. Review it regularly to ensure you are staying on track and adjust it as needed. Life circumstances change, and your budget should reflect those changes.

Tools and Apps for Budgeting

There are many tools and apps available to help you create and manage your budget. Here are some popular options:

1. Mint: Mint is a free app that helps you track your spending, set budgets, and monitor your financial goals. It syncs with your bank accounts and credit cards to provide a comprehensive view of your finances.
2. You Need a Budget (YNAB): YNAB is a popular budgeting app that focuses on helping you give every dollar a job. It encourages proactive budgeting and offers tools to help you pay off debt, save money, and break the paycheck-to-paycheck cycle. It requires a subscription but offers a free trial.
3. EveryDollar: EveryDollar is a user-friendly budgeting app that follows the zero-based budgeting method. The basic version is free, but there's a paid version

that offers additional features like bank account syncing.

4. Personal Capital: Personal Capital offers both budgeting tools and investment tracking. It provides a comprehensive view of your financial health, including net worth, cash flow, and retirement planning. The app is free, with optional advisory services available for a fee.

5. Goodbudget: Goodbudget uses the envelope budgeting method, where you allocate money for different spending categories (envelopes). It's available in both free and paid versions and is suitable for those who prefer a straightforward approach to budgeting.

6. PocketGuard: PocketGuard helps you keep an eye on your spending by showing you how much disposable income you have after accounting for bills, goals, and necessities. It connects to your bank accounts to provide real-time updates and is available in both free and paid versions.

7. Excel or Google Sheets: If you prefer a more hands-on approach, you can create a budget using Excel or Google Sheets. There are many free templates available online that can help you get started.

CHAPTER FOUR

SAVING MONEY

Importance of Saving

Saving money is a fundamental aspect of financial health. It provides a safety net for unexpected expenses, helps you achieve financial goals, and ensures a secure future. Here are some key reasons why saving is important:

1. Financial Security: Having savings provides financial stability and peace of mind. It ensures that you have funds available in case of emergencies, such as medical bills, car repairs, or job loss. This reduces stress and allows you to handle unexpected events without resorting to debt.

2.   Achieving Goals: Savings enable you to reach your financial goals, whether it's buying a home, taking a vacation, paying for education, or starting a business. By setting aside money regularly, you can gradually accumulate the funds needed to achieve these goals.

3.   Building Wealth: Saving is the first step towards investing and building wealth. Once you have a solid savings foundation, you can start investing in assets like stocks, bonds, or real estate to grow your money over time.

4.   Retirement Planning: Saving for retirement ensures that you can maintain your standard of living after you stop working. Contributing to

retirement accounts like a 401(k) or IRA allows your money to grow tax-deferred, providing a comfortable nest egg for your later years.

5. Avoiding Debt: Having savings means you're less likely to rely on credit cards or loans to cover expenses. This helps you avoid high-interest debt and the financial strain that comes with it.

Strategies for Effective Saving

Effective saving requires discipline and smart financial practices. Here are some strategies to help you save money consistently:

1. Pay Yourself First: Treat your savings like a bill that needs to be paid each month. Set up automatic transfers from your checking account to your

savings account as soon as you receive your paycheck. This ensures that you prioritize saving and reduce the temptation to spend the money.

2. Create a Budget: A budget helps you track your income and expenses, making it easier to identify areas where you can cut back and save more. Allocate a specific percentage of your income to savings each month and stick to it.

3. Cut Unnecessary Expenses: Review your spending habits and identify non-essential expenses that you can reduce or eliminate. This might include dining out, subscription services, or impulse purchases. Redirect the money saved

from these cutbacks to your savings account.

4. Set Savings Goals: Having clear, achievable savings goals keeps you motivated and focused. Whether it's a short-term goal like saving for a vacation or a long-term goal like buying a house, knowing what you're saving for makes it easier to stay on track.

5. Use Savings Challenges: Savings challenges can make saving money fun and rewarding. For example, the 52-week savings challenge involves saving a small amount each week, gradually increasing the amount. At the end of the year, you'll have a significant sum saved.

6. Take Advantage of Discounts and Deals: Look for discounts, coupons, and

deals to save money on everyday purchases. Shopping during sales, using cashback apps, and taking advantage of loyalty programs can help you save without sacrificing your lifestyle.

7. Save Windfalls and Bonuses: Whenever you receive extra money, such as tax refunds, bonuses, or gifts, save a portion of it rather than spending it all. This boosts your savings without affecting your regular budget.

Emergency Funds: Why You Need One

An emergency fund is a crucial component of financial security. It is a separate savings account specifically set aside to cover unexpected expenses.

Here's why you need an emergency fund:

1. Protection Against Unexpected Expenses: Life is unpredictable, and unexpected expenses can arise at any time. An emergency fund provides a financial cushion to cover these costs, such as medical emergencies, car repairs, or home maintenance.

2. Avoiding Debt: Without an emergency fund, you might be forced to use credit cards or take out loans to cover unexpected expenses. This can lead to high-interest debt and financial stress. An emergency fund allows you to handle emergencies without relying on borrowed money.

3. Peace of Mind: Knowing that you have money set aside for emergencies gives you peace of mind. It reduces anxiety about potential financial crises and allows you to focus on other aspects of your life without constantly worrying about money.

4. Job Loss Security: In case of job loss or a reduction in income, an emergency fund can help you cover your living expenses while you search for new employment. This financial buffer prevents you from depleting your savings or going into debt during tough times.

5. Flexibility and Control: An emergency fund gives you the flexibility to make better financial decisions.

Without the pressure of an immediate financial crisis, you can take your time to explore options and choose the best course of action for your situation.

Building an Emergency Fund:

1. Determine the Amount: Aim to save three to six months' worth of living expenses. This amount should cover essentials like rent, utilities, groceries, and insurance. If you have dependents or an unstable income, consider saving more.

2. Start Small and Build Gradually: If saving several months' worth of expenses seems overwhelming, start with a smaller goal, like $500 or $1,000, and gradually build up. Consistent

contributions, no matter how small, will add up over time.

3. Keep It Separate: Maintain your emergency fund in a separate, easily accessible savings account. This prevents you from using the money for non-emergencies and ensures it's available when you need it.

4. Automate Savings: Set up automatic transfers to your emergency fund to ensure consistent contributions. Treat it like any other bill you have to pay.

5. Replenish After Use: If you need to dip into your emergency fund, make it a priority to replenish it as soon as possible. This ensures that you are always prepared for future emergencies.

CHAPTER FIVE

DEBT MANAGEMENT

Understanding Different Types of Debt

Debt can be categorized into several types, each with its own characteristics and implications for your financial health. Understanding these different types can help you manage your debt more effectively.

1. Credit Card Debt: This is unsecured debt that accrues when you use credit cards for purchases and carry a balance from month to month. Credit card debt typically comes with high interest rates, which can make it difficult to pay off if not managed carefully.

2. Personal Loans: These are unsecured loans that you can use for various purposes, such as consolidating debt, making large purchases, or covering unexpected expenses. Personal loans usually have fixed interest rates and repayment terms.

3. Student Loans: These are loans taken out to pay for education expenses. They can be federal or private. Federal student loans often have lower interest rates and more flexible repayment options compared to private student loans.

4. Mortgages: This is secured debt used to purchase a home. Mortgages typically have lower interest rates compared to unsecured loans because

the property serves as collateral. Repayment terms can range from 15 to 30 years.

5. Auto Loans: These are secured loans used to purchase vehicles. The vehicle serves as collateral, which usually results in lower interest rates compared to unsecured loans. Repayment terms typically range from 3 to 7 years.

6. Payday Loans: These are short-term, high-interest loans intended to cover expenses until your next payday. Due to their extremely high interest rates and fees, payday loans can lead to a cycle of debt if not repaid quickly.

Understanding the type of debt you have is crucial because it influences the strategies you should use to manage and pay off that debt effectively.

Strategies to Pay Off Debt

Paying off debt requires a strategic approach to ensure you can manage your finances while reducing your debt load. Here are some effective strategies:

1. Debt Snowball Method: This strategy involves paying off your smallest debts first while making minimum payments on larger debts. As each small debt is paid off, you use the money you were paying on it to tackle the next smallest debt. This method can provide quick wins and motivation to keep going.

2. Debt Avalanche Method: With this approach, you prioritize paying off debts

with the highest interest rates first while making minimum payments on lower-interest debts. This method can save you more money in interest over time, although it may take longer to see progress.

3. Debt Consolidation: This involves combining multiple debts into a single loan with a lower interest rate. This can simplify payments and potentially reduce the total amount of interest you pay. Common methods include taking out a personal loan or using a balance transfer credit card.

4. Refinancing: For secured debts like mortgages or auto loans, refinancing can help you obtain a lower interest rate or better repayment terms. This can reduce

your monthly payments and overall interest costs.

5. Negotiating with Creditors: Sometimes, creditors may be willing to negotiate lower interest rates or settlement amounts. Contact your creditors to discuss your situation and explore options for reducing your debt burden.

6. Increasing Your Income: Finding ways to increase your income, such as taking on a side job or freelance work, can provide additional funds to pay down debt faster.

7. Cutting Expenses: Review your budget to identify non-essential expenses you can cut or reduce. Redirect these funds toward paying off your debt.

8. Using Windfalls Wisely: Apply any unexpected money, such as tax refunds, bonuses, or gifts, directly to your debt to reduce the balance more quickly.

Avoiding Debt in the Future

Once you've managed to pay off your debt, it's important to take steps to avoid falling back into debt. Here are some strategies to help you stay debt-free:

1. Create and Stick to a Budget: A budget helps you manage your money effectively, ensuring that you live within your means and avoid overspending. Regularly review and adjust your budget as needed.

2. Build an Emergency Fund: Having an emergency fund provides a financial

buffer for unexpected expenses, reducing the need to rely on credit cards or loans. Aim to save three to six months' worth of living expenses.

3. Use Credit Cards Wisely: If you use credit cards, pay off the balance in full each month to avoid interest charges. Only charge what you can afford to pay off by the due date.

4. Limit Unnecessary Debt: Avoid taking on new debt for non-essential purchases. Before making a purchase, ask yourself if it's something you need and if you can afford it without using credit.

5. Monitor Your Spending: Keep track of your spending to ensure you stay within your budget. Use apps or tools

that help you monitor your expenses and alert you if you're approaching your limits.

6. Plan for Large Expenses: Anticipate large expenses, such as home repairs or vacations, and save for them in advance. This helps you avoid using credit to cover these costs.

7. Stay Educated About Personal Finance: Continuously educate yourself about personal finance to make informed decisions. Read books, take courses, and follow financial experts to stay updated on best practices.

8. Seek Professional Advice: If you're unsure about your financial situation or need help planning, consider consulting a financial advisor. They can provide

personalized advice and help you develop a plan to stay debt-free.

CHAPTER SIX
INCREASING YOUR INCOME

Increasing your income is a powerful way to enhance your financial stability and accelerate the achievement of your financial goals. Here are three effective strategies: finding side hustles, negotiating salary increases, and building multiple streams of income.

Finding Side Hustles

A side hustle is a way to earn extra money outside of your regular job. It can be a great way to boost your income without making major changes to your lifestyle. Here's how to find and start a side hustle:

1. Identify Your Skills and Interests: Think about what you're good at or what

you enjoy doing. Your side hustle should be something you can do well and find fulfilling. Common side hustles include freelance writing, graphic design, tutoring, pet sitting, and ride-sharing.

2. Research Opportunities: Look for side hustle opportunities that match your skills and interests. Websites like Upwork, Fiverr, and TaskRabbit can help you find freelance gigs. For physical tasks or local services, consider advertising in community groups or using platforms like Craigslist.

3. Consider Your Schedule: Choose a side hustle that fits into your existing schedule. If you work a 9-to-5 job, you might look for evening or weekend opportunities. Make sure it's something

you can manage without overwhelming yourself.

4. Start Small: Begin with small projects to build your reputation and experience. As you gain confidence and expertise, you can take on larger projects or increase your rates.

5. Network and Market Yourself: Let people know about your side hustle. Use social media, networking events, and word-of-mouth to spread the word. Building a good reputation and client base can lead to more opportunities.

6. Track Your Earnings and Expenses: Keep a record of your side hustle income and any related expenses. This will help you understand how much you're making and manage your taxes properly.

Negotiating Salary Increases

Negotiating a salary increase can significantly boost your income. Here's how to effectively negotiate for a higher salary:

1. Research Salary Ranges: Find out what others in your position and industry are earning. Websites like Glassdoor, Payscale, and LinkedIn can provide valuable salary data. This information will help you set realistic expectations and justify your request.

2. Prepare Your Case: List your achievements, contributions, and any additional responsibilities you've taken on. Highlight how your work has benefited the company, such as

increasing revenue, improving processes, or saving costs.

3. Choose the Right Time: Timing is important when asking for a raise. Ideally, approach your manager during performance reviews, after completing a successful project, or when the company is performing well financially.

4. Practice Your Pitch: Rehearse what you plan to say during the negotiation. Be confident but respectful. Focus on your value to the company and use specific examples to support your request.

5. Be Open to Negotiation: Your employer might not agree to your initial request but may offer a smaller raise or other benefits like additional vacation

days or a flexible work schedule. Be prepared to discuss alternatives and find a compromise.

6. Follow Up: If your request is denied, ask for feedback and what you can do to qualify for a raise in the future. Set a timeline for revisiting the conversation and take actionable steps to meet the necessary criteria.

Building Multiple Streams of Income

Having multiple streams of income can provide financial security and increase your wealth over time. Here's how to develop and manage multiple income sources:

1. Diversify Your Skills: Invest in learning new skills that can open up

different income opportunities. This might involve taking courses, earning certifications, or gaining experience in new areas.

2. Invest in the Stock Market: Investing in stocks, bonds, or mutual funds can generate passive income through dividends and capital gains. Start with a diversified portfolio and consider consulting a financial advisor to create an investment strategy that aligns with your goals.

3. Real Estate Investments: Real estate can provide rental income and long-term appreciation. You can invest in rental properties, commercial real estate, or Real Estate Investment Trusts (REITs). Make sure to research the

market and understand the responsibilities of property management.

4. Start a Small Business: If you have a business idea, consider starting a small business. This could be an online store, a consulting service, or a local shop. Starting small and gradually expanding can help manage risk and build a steady income stream.

5. Create Passive Income Streams: Look for ways to earn money with minimal ongoing effort. Examples include creating digital products (like e-books or online courses), earning royalties from creative work (such as music or writing), or affiliate marketing.

6. Freelancing and Contract Work: If you have marketable skills, freelancing can provide additional income. Platforms like Upwork, Freelancer, and Fiverr can connect you with clients looking for various services. Freelancing allows you to work on diverse projects and set your own rates.

7. Monetize a Hobby: Turn a hobby or passion into a source of income. Whether it's crafting, photography, or blogging, there are many ways to monetize your interests. Selling products on Etsy, offering photography sessions, or running a monetized blog can generate extra income.

CHAPTER SEVEN
INVESTING

Investing is a key strategy for building wealth and securing your financial future. Understanding the basics, exploring different types of investments, learning how to build an investment portfolio, and managing risk are essential steps in becoming a successful investor.

Basics of Investing

Investing involves putting your money into assets with the expectation of earning a return over time. Here are some fundamental concepts:

1. Return on Investment (ROI): This measures the gain or loss of an investment relative to its cost. ROI is

typically expressed as a percentage and helps evaluate the efficiency of an investment.

2. Compounding: This is the process where the earnings on an investment generate additional earnings. Compounding allows your money to grow faster over time, as you earn returns on both your initial investment and the accumulated earnings.

3. Diversification: This is a risk management strategy that involves spreading your investments across different asset classes and sectors to reduce risk. Diversification helps protect your portfolio from significant losses if one investment performs poorly.

4. Time Horizon: Your time horizon is the length of time you expect to hold an investment before needing to access the funds. Generally, longer time horizons allow for more aggressive investment strategies, as there's more time to recover from market fluctuations.

5. Risk Tolerance: This refers to your ability and willingness to endure market volatility and potential losses. Understanding your risk tolerance helps guide your investment choices and strategy.

Different Types of Investments

There are several types of investments, each with its own characteristics, risks, and potential returns:

1. Stocks: When you buy stocks, you purchase ownership shares in a company. Stocks offer the potential for high returns, but they also come with higher risk. Stock prices can fluctuate significantly based on the company's performance and market conditions.

2. Bonds: Bonds are loans made to corporations or governments in exchange for periodic interest payments and the return of the principal amount at maturity. Bonds are generally considered safer than stocks but offer lower potential returns.

3. Mutual Funds: These are investment vehicles that pool money from many investors to purchase a diversified portfolio of stocks, bonds, or

other assets. Mutual funds provide diversification and professional management but may come with fees and expenses.

4. Exchange-Traded Funds (ETFs): Similar to mutual funds, ETFs hold a diversified portfolio of assets. However, ETFs are traded on stock exchanges like individual stocks, offering greater flexibility and typically lower fees.

5. Real Estate: Investing in real estate involves purchasing property to generate rental income or profit from appreciation. Real estate can provide steady cash flow and long-term growth but requires significant capital and management.

6. Commodities: These are physical goods like gold, silver, oil, and agricultural products. Investing in commodities can provide diversification and act as a hedge against inflation, but prices can be volatile.

7. Cryptocurrencies: Digital currencies like Bitcoin and Ethereum are relatively new and highly volatile investments. Cryptocurrencies offer the potential for high returns but come with significant risk and regulatory uncertainty.

8. Certificates of Deposit (CDs): CDs are time deposits offered by banks that pay a fixed interest rate for a specified term. They are low-risk investments but

offer lower returns compared to stocks or bonds.

Building an Investment Portfolio

Creating a well-balanced investment portfolio involves several steps:

1. Determine Your Goals: Identify your financial goals, such as retirement, buying a home, or funding education. Your goals will help shape your investment strategy and time horizon.

2. Assess Your Risk Tolerance: Understand how much risk you're willing to take. This will influence the mix of assets in your portfolio. Generally, younger investors can afford to take more risk, while those nearing retirement might prefer a more conservative approach.

3. Allocate Assets: Decide how to divide your investments among different asset classes (stocks, bonds, real estate, etc.). This is called asset allocation and is crucial for managing risk and achieving your goals. A common rule of thumb is to subtract your age from 100 to determine the percentage of your portfolio that should be in stocks.

4. Diversify: Within each asset class, diversify your investments to spread risk. For example, if you invest in stocks, choose a mix of companies from different industries and geographical regions.

5. Choose Investment Vehicles: Select specific investments that fit your asset allocation and diversification strategy.

This might include individual stocks, mutual funds, ETFs, or bonds.

6. Monitor and Rebalance: Regularly review your portfolio to ensure it remains aligned with your goals and risk tolerance. Rebalance periodically by adjusting your investments to maintain your desired asset allocation.

Risk Management in Investing

Managing risk is crucial to protecting your investments and achieving long-term success. Here are some strategies:

1. Diversification: As mentioned earlier, spreading your investments across various assets reduces the impact of poor performance in any single investment.

2. Asset Allocation: Allocate your investments based on your risk tolerance and time horizon. A balanced mix of stocks, bonds, and other assets can provide growth potential while reducing risk.

3. Regular Monitoring: Keep an eye on your investments and the overall market. Regularly reviewing your portfolio helps you stay informed and make necessary adjustments.

4. Avoid Emotional Decisions: Market fluctuations can lead to emotional decision-making. Stick to your long-term strategy and avoid reacting impulsively to short-term market movements.

5. Use Stop-Loss Orders: For stock investments, consider using stop-loss orders to automatically sell a stock if its price falls to a certain level. This can help limit losses.

6. Stay Informed: Continuously educate yourself about investing. Understanding market trends, economic indicators, and financial news can help you make informed decisions.

7. Seek Professional Advice: If you're unsure about your investment strategy, consider consulting a financial advisor. They can provide personalized guidance based on your financial situation and goals.

CHAPTER EIGHT
BUILDING PASSIVE INCOME

Building passive income is an excellent way to achieve financial independence and create a steady cash flow with minimal ongoing effort. Understanding what passive income is, exploring different sources, and implementing strategies to build passive income streams can help you secure your financial future.

What is Passive Income?

Passive income is money earned with little to no active involvement on your part. Unlike active income, where you trade time for money (like a regular job), passive income requires an initial investment of time, money, or effort, after which it generates revenue on its own. The goal is to create sources of income that continue to pay you without needing constant attention.

Different Sources of Passive Income

There are numerous ways to generate passive income, each with its own requirements and potential returns. Here are some common sources:

1. Real Estate Investments:

A. Rental Properties: Owning rental properties can provide a steady stream of income through monthly rent payments. While managing tenants and property maintenance requires some effort, it can be minimized with a property management service.

B. Real Estate Investment Trusts (REITs): Investing in REITs allows you to earn income from real estate without owning physical properties. REITs pay dividends to investors from the rental income and profits from real estate holdings.

2. Dividend Stocks:

A. Investing in dividend-paying stocks allows you to earn regular income from company profits. Many established companies distribute a portion of their earnings to shareholders in the form of dividends.

3. Peer-to-Peer Lending:

A. Platforms like LendingClub or Prosper let you lend money to individuals or small businesses in exchange for interest payments. While there is some risk involved, diversifying your loans across multiple borrowers can mitigate it.

4. Royalties:

A. If you have creative skills, you can earn royalties from books, music, patents, or other intellectual property. For example, authors earn royalties from book sales, and musicians earn from album sales or streaming services.

5. Online Businesses and E-commerce:

A. Creating an online store or business can generate passive income, especially if it operates on an automated platform. Dropshipping, where you sell products without handling inventory, and print-on-demand services are popular e-commerce models.

6. Digital Products:

A. Selling digital products like e-books, courses, software, or photography can provide passive income. Once created, these products can be sold repeatedly with minimal ongoing effort.

7. Affiliate Marketing:

A. Affiliate marketing involves promoting products or services and earning a commission for each sale made through your referral link. This can be done through blogs, social media, or websites.

8. Savings and Investments:

A. High-Yield Savings Accounts and CDs: These offer modest returns through interest payments. They are low-risk but also provide lower returns compared to other passive income sources.

B. Bonds: Investing in government or corporate bonds can provide regular interest payments. Bonds are generally considered safer than stocks but offer lower returns.

9. Automated Services:

A. Developing apps or websites that provide a service or sell a product can generate passive income. These need initial development and marketing but can earn money with minimal ongoing management.

Strategies to Build Passive Income Streams

Building passive income requires strategic planning and effort. Here are some strategies to help you develop multiple streams of passive income:

1. Start Small and Scale Up:

A. Begin with one or two passive income sources that require minimal investment. As these start generating income, reinvest the profits into additional passive income streams.

2. Leverage Your Skills and Interests:

A. Choose passive income opportunities that align with your skills and interests. This will make the initial setup phase more enjoyable and increase your chances of success.

3. Invest Wisely:

A. Research and choose investments that align with your risk tolerance and financial goals. Diversifying your investments across different asset classes can help manage risk.

4. Automate Where Possible:

A. Use automation tools to reduce the amount of active involvement required. For example, use scheduling tools for online businesses, automate investment contributions, or hire property managers for rental properties.

5. Focus on High-Quality Assets:

A. Invest in high-quality assets that have the potential to generate consistent and reliable income. This might include blue-chip stocks, well-maintained rental properties, or high-demand digital products.

6. Monitor and Adjust:

A. Regularly review the performance of your passive income streams. Be prepared to make adjustments as needed, whether it's tweaking your investment portfolio, updating digital products, or changing your marketing strategies.

7. Reinvest Earnings:

A. Reinvest the earnings from your passive income sources to grow your income over time. For example, use dividends to purchase more stocks, or profits from a digital product to create new products.

8. Educate Yourself Continuously:

A. Stay informed about new passive income opportunities and best practices. Read books, take courses, and follow experts in the field to continuously improve your knowledge and strategies.

CHAPTER NINE
ENTREPRENEURSHIP

Starting your own business is an exciting and challenging path to financial independence and personal fulfillment. Understanding how to start a business from scratch, identifying business ideas with low start-up costs, and learning how to scale your business are essential steps for successful entrepreneurship.

Starting a Business from Scratch

Starting a business from scratch involves several key steps:

1. Identify a Viable Business Idea:

A. Begin by identifying a problem you can solve or a need you can fulfill. Consider your skills, interests, and market demand. Your business idea should be something you are passionate about and have the expertise to pursue.

2. Conduct Market Research:

A. Research your target market to understand your potential customers, competitors, and industry trends. This helps you validate your business idea and identify opportunities and challenges.

3. Create a Business Plan:

A. A business plan outlines your business goals, target market, marketing strategy, financial projections, and operational plan. It serves as a roadmap for your business and is essential if you seek funding from investors or lenders.

4. Choose a Business Structure:

A. Decide on the legal structure of your business, such as a sole proprietorship, partnership, corporation, or LLC. Each structure has different legal and tax implications, so choose the one that best suits your needs.

5. Register Your Business:

A. Register your business name and obtain any necessary licenses or permits. This ensures your business operates legally and complies with local, state, and federal regulations.

6. Set Up Your Finances:

A. Open a separate business bank account and set up accounting systems to track your income and expenses. Consider hiring an accountant or using accounting software to manage your finances effectively.

7. Develop Your Product or Service:

A. Create a prototype or minimum viable product (MVP) to test your idea. Gather feedback from potential customers and refine your product or service based on their input.

8. Launch and Market Your Business:

A. Launch your business with a marketing strategy to attract customers. Use a mix of online and offline marketing techniques, such as social media, email marketing, content marketing, and local advertising.

9. Build a Customer Base:

A. Focus on providing excellent customer service to build a loyal customer base. Encourage customer reviews and referrals to grow your business through word-of-mouth.

Business Ideas with Low Start-Up Costs

Starting a business doesn't always require significant capital. Here are some business ideas with low start-up costs:

1. Freelancing:

A. Offer your skills and services as a freelancer. This could include writing, graphic design, web development, marketing, or consulting. Freelancing platforms like Upwork and Fiverr can help you find clients.

2. Online Store:

A. Set up an online store using platforms like Shopify or Etsy to sell handmade goods, vintage items, or dropshipped products. With minimal inventory and overhead costs, an online store can be a cost-effective business model.

3. Blogging or Vlogging:

A. Create a blog or YouTube channel focused on a niche topic you're passionate about. Monetize through ads, sponsored content, affiliate marketing, or selling your own products.

4. Virtual Assistant:

A. Provide administrative support to businesses or entrepreneurs remotely. Services can include email management, scheduling, social media management, and customer service.

5. Tutoring or Coaching:

A. Offer tutoring services in subjects you excel in or coaching in areas like fitness, business, or life skills. You can conduct sessions online or in-person.

6. Pet Sitting or Dog Walking:

A. Provide pet care services such as pet sitting, dog walking, or grooming. This business can be started with minimal equipment and marketing.

7. Home Cleaning Services:

A. Offer home cleaning or organizing services. This business requires basic cleaning supplies and can be marketed through local advertising and word-of-mouth.

8. Print-on-Demand:

A. Create custom designs for products like t-shirts, mugs, or phone cases and sell them through print-on-demand services. This eliminates the need for inventory and reduces upfront costs.

9. Event Planning:

A. Plan and coordinate events such as weddings, parties, or corporate functions. Use your organizational skills and network to build a client base.

Scaling Your Business

Scaling your business involves growing your operations to increase revenue and reach a larger market. Here are strategies to scale your business effectively:

1. Standardize Processes:

A. Develop standard operating procedures (SOPs) for key tasks to ensure consistency and efficiency. This makes it easier to train new employees and maintain quality as you grow.

2. Automate and Delegate:

A. Use automation tools to streamline repetitive tasks, such as email marketing, invoicing, and customer relationship management (CRM). Delegate tasks to employees or outsource them to free up your time for strategic planning.

3. Expand Your Product or Service Line:

A. Introduce new products or services that complement your existing offerings. This can attract new customers and increase sales from existing customers.

4. Increase Your Marketing Efforts:

A. Invest in marketing to reach a wider audience. Use a mix of digital marketing strategies, such as search engine optimization (SEO), pay-per-click (PPC) advertising, social media marketing, and content marketing.

5. Leverage Technology:

A. Implement technology solutions to improve efficiency and scalability. This could include e-commerce platforms, customer service software, and project management tools.

6. Focus on Customer Retention:

A. Building long-term relationships with customers can lead to repeat business and referrals. Implement loyalty programs, provide exceptional customer service, and regularly engage with your customers.

7. Seek Funding:

A. To scale quickly, you might need additional capital. Explore funding options like small business loans, venture capital, or crowdfunding to finance your growth.

8. Hire the Right Team:

A. As your business grows, hiring skilled employees is crucial. Focus on building a team that aligns with your business values and goals. Invest in their training and development to ensure they contribute effectively to your growth.

9. Monitor and Adjust:

A. Continuously monitor your business performance and market trends. Be prepared to pivot or adjust your strategy as needed to stay competitive and capitalize on new opportunities.

CHAPTER TEN

NETWORKING AND MENTORSHIP

Building a strong network and seeking mentorship are crucial for personal and professional growth. They can provide invaluable support, guidance, and opportunities. Understanding the importance of networking, finding and working with mentors, and leveraging relationships for financial growth can significantly enhance your journey to success.

The Importance of Networking

Networking is about building and maintaining professional relationships that can provide mutual benefits. Here's why networking is essential:

1. Opportunities: Networking can open doors to new job opportunities, business partnerships, and collaborations. Many positions are filled through referrals and recommendations within professional networks.

2. Knowledge Sharing: Engaging with others in your industry allows you to exchange ideas, share experiences, and stay informed about the latest trends and developments. This collective knowledge can help you make better decisions and stay ahead of the curve.

3. Support System: A strong network provides a support system of peers and mentors who can offer advice, encouragement, and feedback. This support can be especially valuable

during challenging times or when making important decisions.

4. Visibility and Reputation: Actively participating in professional communities can increase your visibility and enhance your reputation. Being known and respected in your field can lead to more opportunities and recognition.

5. Skill Development: Networking events, seminars, and conferences often provide opportunities for learning and skill development. Engaging with experts and thought leaders can help you gain new insights and improve your skills.

Finding and Working with Mentors

Mentors are experienced individuals who can provide guidance, advice, and support based on their own experiences. Here's how to find and work effectively with mentors:

1. Identify Your Needs: Determine what you're looking for in a mentor. This could be specific skills, industry knowledge, career advice, or personal growth. Knowing your needs will help you identify the right mentor.

2. Look for Potential Mentors: Seek out individuals who have the experience and expertise you're looking for. This could be within your existing network, professional organizations, industry

events, or online platforms like LinkedIn.

3. Approach with Respect: When approaching a potential mentor, be respectful and clear about why you're seeking their guidance. Explain what you admire about their experience and how you believe they can help you achieve your goals.

4. Build a Relationship: Mentorship is a two-way relationship. Show genuine interest in your mentor's work and experiences. Be open, honest, and appreciative of their time and advice.

5. Set Clear Expectations: Discuss and agree on the structure of the mentorship, including how often you'll meet, preferred communication

methods, and the specific areas you'd like to focus on. Having clear expectations helps ensure productive and meaningful interactions.

6. Act on Advice: Show your mentor that you value their guidance by taking action on their advice. Implementing their suggestions and providing feedback on your progress demonstrates your commitment and respect for their time.

7. Be Patient and Respect Boundaries: Mentors have their own commitments and limitations. Be patient and respectful of their time and boundaries. A good mentorship relationship evolves naturally and can't be forced.

Leveraging Relationships for Financial Growth

Building and maintaining professional relationships can directly contribute to your financial growth in several ways:

1. Access to Opportunities: Strong relationships can lead to job offers, business deals, and investment opportunities. People are more likely to share opportunities with those they know and trust.

2. Collaborations and Partnerships: Networking can help you find potential business partners and collaborators. Partnerships can expand your reach, share resources, and create synergies that drive growth.

3. Referrals and Recommendations: Satisfied clients, colleagues, and mentors can refer you to new clients, investors, or employers. Referrals carry a level of trust and credibility that can be very beneficial.

4. Learning and Development: Relationships with knowledgeable individuals can help you learn new skills, gain insights, and stay updated with industry trends. Continuous learning and improvement can enhance your career and financial prospects.

5. Negotiation and Bargaining Power: A strong network can provide you with valuable information and leverage during negotiations. Knowing market rates, industry standards, and having

influential contacts can help you negotiate better deals and salaries.

6. Support and Motivation: Professional relationships can provide the support and motivation needed to pursue ambitious goals. Having a network of like-minded individuals can inspire and encourage you to take calculated risks and strive for greater achievements.

7. Access to Resources: Networking can connect you with resources such as funding, talent, and technology. Leveraging these resources can help you grow your business or advance your career.

8. Brand Building: Your network can help you build and promote your

personal or business brand. Positive word-of-mouth and endorsements from respected individuals can significantly enhance your reputation and attract more clients or opportunities.

CHAPTER ELEVEN

FRUGALITY AND SMART SPENDING

Being frugal and practicing smart spending habits are crucial strategies for building and maintaining wealth. By living below your means, adopting intelligent spending habits, and making cost-effective lifestyle choices, you can significantly enhance your financial well-being.

Living Below Your Means

Living below your means means spending less than you earn. It's the foundation of financial stability and wealth accumulation. Here's how to achieve it:

1. Create a Budget:

A. Start by tracking your income and expenses to understand where your money is going. Create a budget that allocates money for essential expenses (like housing, utilities, groceries, and transportation) and savings. Stick to your budget to avoid overspending.

2. Prioritize Savings:

A. Treat savings as a non-negotiable expense. Aim to save at least 20% of your income. Automate transfers to your savings account to ensure consistency. An emergency fund should be a priority, providing a safety net for unexpected expenses.

3. Avoid Debt:

A. Minimize the use of credit cards and loans for non-essential purchases.

High-interest debt can quickly derail your financial goals. If you have existing debt, prioritize paying it off, starting with the highest interest debt.

4. Control Impulse Spending:

A. Avoid making impulse purchases. Before buying something non-essential, wait 24 hours to determine if it's a need or a want. This practice can help you make more thoughtful spending decisions.

5. Embrace a Minimalist Lifestyle:

A. Focus on buying only what you truly need and value. A minimalist approach can help you save money and reduce clutter, leading to a simpler and more fulfilling life.

6. Set Financial Goals:

A. Define clear financial goals, such as saving for retirement, buying a home, or traveling. Having specific goals can motivate you to live frugally and manage your money better.

Smart Spending Habits

Smart spending involves making thoughtful and deliberate decisions about how you use your money. Here are some habits to adopt:

1. Comparison Shopping:

A. Before making a purchase, compare prices from different stores and online platforms to ensure you're getting the best deal. Use price comparison websites and apps to make this process easier.

2. Buy Quality Over Quantity:

A. Investing in high-quality items may cost more upfront but can save you money in the long run. Durable and well-made products last longer and reduce the need for frequent replacements.

3. Use Coupons and Discounts:

A. Take advantage of coupons, discount codes, and sales to save money on purchases. Sign up for newsletters from your favorite stores to receive exclusive deals and promotions.

4. Avoid Lifestyle Inflation:

A. As your income increases, resist the temptation to increase your spending proportionally. Maintain your current lifestyle and use the additional income to boost your savings and investments.

5. Plan Your Meals:

A. Meal planning can help you save money on groceries and reduce food waste. Cook at home more often instead of dining out, and prepare meals in bulk to save time and money.

6. Track Your Spending:

A. Regularly review your spending to identify areas where you can cut back. Use budgeting apps or spreadsheets to monitor your expenses and stay on track with your financial goals.

7. Pay with Cash:

A. Using cash for purchases can help you stay within your budget and reduce the likelihood of overspending. It's easier to see how much money you're spending when you physically hand over cash.

Cost-Effective Lifestyle Choices

Adopting a cost-effective lifestyle can lead to significant savings and financial freedom. Here are some choices to consider:

1. Live in a Affordable Area:

A. Housing is often the largest expense. Consider living in a more affordable area or downsizing your home to reduce housing costs. Evaluate your housing needs and prioritize functionality over luxury.

2. Use Public Transportation:

A. If possible, use public transportation instead of owning a car. Public transport is usually cheaper than the costs associated with car ownership, including maintenance, insurance, and fuel. If you need a car, consider buying a reliable used vehicle instead of a new one.

3. DIY and Repairs:

A. Learn to do basic home repairs and maintenance tasks yourself. DIY projects can save you money on labor costs and give you a sense of accomplishment. There are plenty of online tutorials and resources to help you learn new skills.

4. Reduce Utility Bills:

A. Implement energy-saving measures to reduce utility bills. Simple actions like using energy-efficient appliances, unplugging devices when not in use, and setting your thermostat wisely can lead to significant savings.

5. Buy Secondhand:

A. Consider purchasing secondhand items, such as furniture, clothing, and electronics. Thrift stores, online marketplaces, and garage sales can offer quality items at a fraction of the cost of new ones.

6. Cancel Unnecessary Subscriptions:

A. Review your subscriptions and memberships to identify any that you don't use or need. Canceling these can save you money each month. Consider sharing streaming services with family or friends to split the cost.

7. Exercise Outdoors:

A. Instead of paying for a gym membership, take advantage of outdoor activities like walking, running, or biking. Many communities also offer free or low-cost fitness classes and recreational facilities.

8. Grow Your Own Food:

A. If you have space, start a garden to grow your own fruits and vegetables. Gardening can be a rewarding and cost-effective way to supplement your grocery needs.

9. Entertain at Home:

A. Instead of spending money on expensive outings, entertain friends and family at home. Host potluck dinners, game nights, or movie marathons for a fun and frugal way to socialize.

CHAPTER TWELVE

CONTINUOUS LEARNING AND ADAPTATION

In today's rapidly evolving world, continuous learning and adaptation are essential for personal and professional growth. Whether it's staying updated with financial trends, adapting to changing economic conditions, or simply embracing the importance of lifelong learning, these practices are key to staying relevant, competitive, and successful.

Importance of Lifelong Learning

Lifelong learning refers to the ongoing pursuit of knowledge and skills throughout one's life. Here's why it's crucial:

1. Career Advancement: In today's knowledge-based economy, industries and job roles are constantly evolving. Lifelong learning allows individuals to acquire new skills and stay competitive in their fields, opening up opportunities for career advancement and professional growth.

2. Personal Development: Learning new things can broaden your horizons, stimulate your mind, and enhance your creativity. It provides opportunities for personal enrichment and self-improvement, leading to a more fulfilling and meaningful life.

3. Adaptability: Lifelong learners are better equipped to adapt to change. They embrace new technologies,

methodologies, and ideas with ease, making them more resilient in the face of uncertainty and disruption.

4. Problem Solving: Continuous learning improves critical thinking and problem-solving skills. It enables individuals to approach challenges with a growth mindset, seeking innovative solutions and learning from failures along the way.

5. Increased Confidence: Mastering new skills and knowledge boosts confidence and self-esteem. Lifelong learners are more willing to take on challenges and pursue ambitious goals, knowing they have the capability to learn and grow.

6. Social Connection: Learning often involves interaction with others, whether through classes, workshops, or online communities. Lifelong learning fosters social connections and a sense of belonging, leading to richer and more diverse personal and professional networks.

Staying Updated with Financial Trends

Staying updated with financial trends is crucial for making informed decisions about investments, budgeting, and financial planning. Here's why it matters:

1. Maximizing Opportunities: Financial markets are constantly evolving, influenced by factors such as

economic conditions, geopolitical events, and technological advancements. Staying updated with trends allows investors to identify opportunities and capitalize on them before they become mainstream.

2. Mitigating Risks: Understanding financial trends helps individuals and businesses anticipate and mitigate potential risks. It enables them to adjust their investment portfolios, diversify their assets, and implement risk management strategies to protect their finances.

3. Optimizing Investments: By staying informed about market trends, individuals can make more informed decisions about where to allocate their

funds. Whether it's stocks, bonds, real estate, or alternative investments, staying updated allows investors to optimize their investment portfolios for maximum returns.

4. Financial Planning: Financial trends can impact personal and business finances in significant ways. Staying updated allows individuals to adjust their financial plans accordingly, whether it's saving for retirement, paying off debt, or planning for major expenses like education or healthcare.

5. Adapting to Regulatory Changes: Financial markets are subject to regulatory changes that can affect investment strategies and financial outcomes. Staying updated with

regulatory trends ensures compliance with laws and regulations and minimizes the risk of legal and financial penalties.

6. Competitive Advantage: In today's fast-paced financial landscape, those who stay ahead of the curve have a competitive advantage. By staying updated with financial trends, individuals and businesses can position themselves as industry leaders and innovators, gaining the trust and confidence of clients and stakeholders.

Adapting to Changing Economic Conditions

Economic conditions are constantly changing, influenced by factors such as inflation, interest rates, employment levels, and consumer confidence. Here's why it's essential to adapt:

1. Resilience: Economic downturns and recessions are inevitable parts of the business cycle. Adapting to changing economic conditions allows individuals and businesses to weather the storm, survive challenging times, and emerge stronger on the other side.

2. Opportunistic Investing: Economic fluctuations create opportunities for savvy investors. Adapting to changing economic conditions allows investors to identify undervalued assets, capitalize on market inefficiencies, and generate significant returns over the long term.

3. Strategic Planning: Changing economic conditions require

adjustments to business strategies and plans. Adapting allows businesses to pivot quickly, seize new opportunities, and stay ahead of competitors in dynamic markets.

4. Risk Management: Economic volatility can pose risks to financial stability. Adapting to changing economic conditions involves implementing risk management strategies, such as diversifying revenue streams, maintaining adequate cash reserves, and hedging against currency and commodity price fluctuations.

5. Consumer Behavior: Economic conditions influence consumer behavior, spending patterns, and preferences. Adapting to these changes allows

businesses to tailor their products, services, and marketing strategies to meet evolving consumer needs and preferences, ensuring long-term relevance and competitiveness.

6. Policy Implications: Government policies and regulations play a significant role in shaping economic conditions. Adapting to changes in policy environments allows individuals and businesses to anticipate potential impacts on taxes, regulations, and market dynamics, and adjust their strategies accordingly.

CHAPTER THIRTEEN

PHILANTHROPY AND GIVING BACK

Philanthropy, the act of giving back to society, plays a significant role not only in enriching the lives of others but also in enhancing one's own wealth and well-being. Understanding the role of philanthropy in wealth building and how giving back can contribute to personal and financial growth is essential for individuals seeking to make a positive impact on the world while also securing their own prosperity.

The Role of Philanthropy in Wealth Building

Philanthropy is often viewed as a fundamental aspect of wealth building, and for good reason. Here's why:

1. Social Impact: Philanthropy allows individuals to contribute to causes and organizations that are meaningful to them. By addressing societal issues such as poverty, education, healthcare, and environmental conservation, philanthropy creates positive social change and improves the well-being of communities.

2. Legacy Building: Engaging in philanthropy enables individuals to leave a lasting legacy beyond financial wealth. By supporting causes aligned with their values and passions, philanthropists can make a meaningful impact that extends far into the future, leaving a positive mark on society for generations to come.

3. Network Building: Philanthropy provides opportunities to connect with like-minded individuals, organizations, and community leaders. Building relationships through philanthropic activities can lead to valuable networking opportunities, business partnerships, and collaborations that enhance both personal and professional growth.

4. Tax Benefits: Charitable donations often come with tax benefits. In many countries, individuals who donate to qualified charitable organizations can receive tax deductions or credits, reducing their taxable income and potentially lowering their overall tax liability.

5. Personal Fulfillment: Giving back brings a sense of fulfillment and purpose to individuals. Knowing that their contributions are making a positive difference in the lives of others can boost self-esteem, happiness, and overall well-being, enriching their lives in ways that money alone cannot.

6. Philanthropic Leadership: Engaging in philanthropy can position individuals as leaders and influencers in their communities and industries. By taking an active role in addressing social issues and driving positive change, philanthropists can inspire others to join their efforts and amplify their impact.

How Giving Back Can Enhance Your Wealth

Contrary to popular belief, giving back does not diminish wealth but rather enhances it in various ways:

1. Personal Growth: Giving back fosters personal growth by promoting empathy, compassion, and gratitude. Engaging in philanthropy allows individuals to develop a deeper understanding of social issues and cultivate important character traits such as generosity, kindness, and humility.

2. Enhanced Reputation: Philanthropy can enhance an individual's reputation and credibility, both personally and professionally. By publicly supporting charitable causes

and giving back to their communities, individuals build trust and goodwill among peers, clients, and stakeholders, which can open doors to new opportunities and collaborations.

3. Expanded Networks: Giving back provides opportunities to connect with a diverse range of individuals, including fellow donors, nonprofit leaders, and community members. Building relationships through philanthropy expands one's network, creating valuable connections that can lead to personal and professional growth, mentorship, and support.

4. Leadership Development: Engaging in philanthropy allows individuals to develop leadership skills

and qualities such as strategic thinking, decision-making, and problem-solving. By taking an active role in philanthropic initiatives, individuals can hone their leadership abilities and make a meaningful impact on the causes they care about.

5. Business Benefits: Giving back can have positive effects on businesses as well. Corporate philanthropy, such as corporate social responsibility (CSR) initiatives and charitable partnerships, can enhance brand reputation, customer loyalty, and employee morale, ultimately contributing to long-term business success and profitability.

6. Psychological Wealth: True wealth encompasses more than just financial

assets; it includes factors such as health, relationships, and personal fulfillment. Giving back contributes to psychological wealth by promoting happiness, fulfillment, and a sense of purpose, which are invaluable aspects of overall well-being and quality of life.

7. Legacy and Impact: Giving back allows individuals to leave a meaningful legacy that extends beyond material wealth. By supporting causes and organizations that align with their values and passions, individuals can make a lasting impact on society and future generations, ensuring that their contributions live on long after they are gone.

THE END

www.ingramcontent.com/pod-product-compliance
Lightning Source LLC
Chambersburg PA
CBHW052321220526
45472CB00001B/212